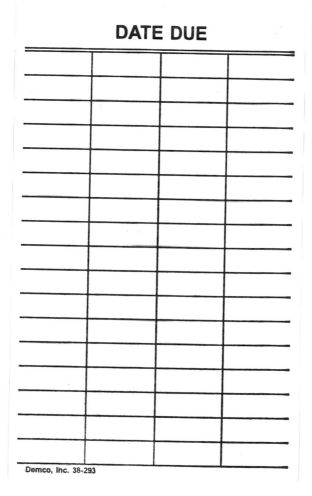

DATE DUE

Demco, Inc. 38-293

READING POWER

Women Who Shaped History

Katharine Graham
and 20th Century
American Journalism

Joanne Mattern

The Rosen Publishing Group's

PowerKids Press™
New York

Published in 2003 by The Rosen Publishing Group, Inc.
29 East 21st Street, New York, NY 10010

First Edition

Book Design: Erica Clendening

Photo Credits: Cover, pp. 10–11, 12–13, 13 (inset), 15, 17 (top and bottom), 20, 21 © AP/Wide World; p. 4 (map) Erica Clendening; p. 5 Library of Congress, Prints and Photographs Divison; pp. 6, 9 (top) © Hank Walter/Timepix; p. 7 © The Graham Family; p. 9 (bottom) © Walter Bennet/TimePix; pp. 14, 18 Adriana Skura; p. 19 © 2001, *The Washington Post*. Photo by Robert A. Reeder. Reprinted with permission

Library of Congress Cataloging-in-Publication Data

Mattern, Joanne, 1963-
Katharine Graham and 20th century American journalism / Joanne Mattern.
    p. cm. — (Women who shaped history)
Summary: A brief biography of the Pulitzer Prize-winning author and Washington Post publisher who helped lead the newspaper's coverage of the Watergate scandal.
Includes bibliographical references and index.
ISBN 0-8239-6500-7 (lib. bdg.)
1. Graham, Katharine, 1917—Juvenile literature. 2. Publishers and publishing—United States—Biography—Juvenile literature. 3. Washington post (Washington, D.C. : 1974)—History—Juvenile literature. 4. Newspaper publishing—Washington (D.C.)—History—20th century—Juvenile literature. [1. Graham, Katharine, 1917- 2. Publishers and publishing. 3. Washington post (Washington, D.C. : 1974) 4. Newspaper publishing. 5. Women—Biography.] I. Title.
Z473.G7 M38 2003
070'.5'092—dc21

                                    2002000510

Contents

Who Was Katharine Graham?   4

School Days   6

Family Life   8

The Washington Post   10

After the *Post*   16

Glossary   22

Resources   23

Index/Word Count   24

Note   24

Katharine Graham owned and operated one of the most important newspapers in the world. The stories in her newspaper changed the world.

Katharine Meyer (Graham) was born in New York City on June 16, 1917. She grew up in Washington, D.C.

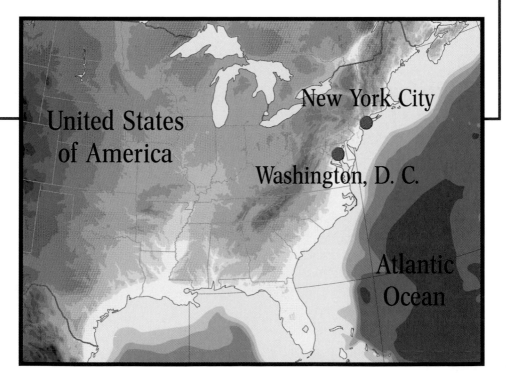

As a child, Katharine enjoyed riding horses.

When Katharine was in high school, her father bought *The Washington Post* newspaper. She started working at the *Post* a year after she finished college. She helped to edit the newspaper.

Eugene Meyer, Katharine's father, was very successful. He bought the *Times Herald* and made it a part of *The Washington Post*.

Katharine graduated from the Medeira School. It was a very good high school for girls.

7

In 1940, Katharine Meyer married Philip Graham. They had four children— Elizabeth, Donald, William, and Stephen.

Katharine's father asked Philip Graham to work at the *Post*. Soon, Katharine's father gave control of the *Post* to her husband. She stayed home to raise the children.

In 1963, Philip Graham died and Katharine Graham became president of the *Post*.

Katharine (far left); her husband, Philip (far right); and Katharine's parents discuss *The Washington Post.*

(From left to right) The Graham family — Elizabeth, Katharine, Philip, Stephen, William, and Donald — get together for a family photo.

Many people thought Katharine Graham would sell *The Washington Post* after her husband died. They didn't think that a woman could run a newspaper as well as a man could.

Katharine Graham was often the only woman at important business meetings.

However, Graham didn't sell the *Post*. She decided to run it herself.

Katharine Graham had to learn how to run a newspaper. She studied hard and asked her friends for help.

"She set the newspaper on a course that took it to the very top ranks of American journalism."

—Ben Bradlee, *Post* executive editor

In 1972, two *Post* reporters, Bob Woodward and Carl Bernstein, started writing stories about a break-in at the Watergate Hotel in Washington, D.C. They learned that people in the government had done it. These people were trying to spy on others in the government.

Reporters Bob Woodward (left) and Carl Bernstein (right) worked to find out the truth about the Watergate break-in.

The Watergate Hotel was the scene of the break-in.

13

Many powerful people tried to stop the *Post* from printing the stories about the Watergate break-in. Katharine Graham believed that Americans needed to know the truth. She kept printing the stories. The *Post* found out that President Richard Nixon was breaking the law, too.

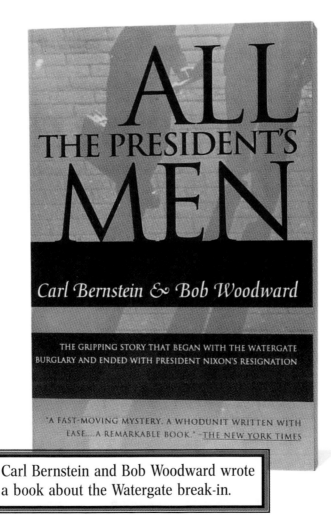

Carl Bernstein and Bob Woodward wrote a book about the Watergate break-in.

In 1974, President Nixon left his job as president of the United States because he told people to do something that was against the law.

In 1979, Katharine Graham gave the job of running *The Washington Post* to her son, Donald Graham. However, she still kept very busy. Graham helped to make decisions for the *Post*, several television stations, and a newsmagazine. She also worked with many charities.

Katharine Graham (shown here in 1991) worked closely with her son Donald Graham (left) and *Post* editor Ben Bradlee (right) on important matters.

In 2001, Katharine Graham accepted an award for her work on *The Washington Post.*

Katharine Graham also became a respected writer. She wrote a book about her life called *Personal History*.

In 1998, Katharine Graham won the Pulitzer Prize, a very famous award given to American writers.

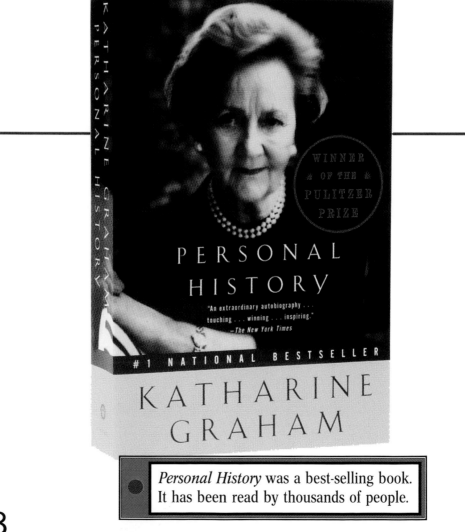

Personal History was a best-selling book. It has been read by thousands of people.

Katharine Graham was very happy to receive the Pulitzer Prize for her book.

Now You Know

Katharine Graham was eighty years old when she won the Pulitzer Prize.

Katharine Graham died on July 17, 2001. She was eighty-four years old.

Katharine Graham set an example for people everywhere. She fought for freedom of the press. She believed in telling Americans the truth when no one else would. Katharine Graham's hard work and courage made her one of the most powerful people in American journalism.

Time Line

June 16, 1917
Katharine Meyer is born

1940 *Marries Philip Graham*

1945 *Son Donald Graham is born*

1934 *Graduates from the Madeira School*

1943 *Daughter Elizabeth Graham is born*

1948 *Son William Graham is born*

Katharine Graham met many important people. Here, Vice President Al Gore (left) gives Graham a medal for her work.

1952 Son Stephen Graham is born

1963 Philip Graham dies and Katharine Graham takes control of the Post

1971 The Post prints the Pentagon Papers

1972–1974 The Post prints stories about the Watergate break-in

1979 Katharine Graham's son Donald Graham takes over running the Post

July 17, 2001 Katharine Graham dies in Sun Valley, Idaho

1998 Wins Pulitzer Prize for Personal History

Glossary

charities (**char**-uh-teez) groups that raise money for people in need

edit (**ehd**-iht) to check a piece of writing for mistakes

editor (**ehd**-uh-tuhr) someone who decides what will be printed in a newspaper, magazine, book, or on a Web site

graduated (**graj**-oo-ayt-uhd) having finished a course of study at a school or college

journalism (**jehr**-nehl-ihz-uhm) the work of gathering, writing, and reporting news for newspapers, magazines, or other media

newsmagazine (**nooz**-mag-uh-zeen) a magazine or TV program that only runs news stories

Pentagon Papers (**pehn**-tuh-gahn **pay**-puhrz) top secret information about the United States and the Vietnam War

Pulitzer Prize (**pu**-luht-suhr **pryz**) a very famous award for journalism, literature, drama, and music

reporters (rih-**pohr**-tuhrz) people who gather information and write stories for newspapers, magazines, or television or radio stations

spy (**spy**) to watch someone closely from a hidden place, secretly collecting information

Resources

Books

*Let's Go! Let's Publish: Katharine Graham
and the Washington Post*
by Nancy Whitelaw
Morgan Reynolds (1999)

Women Who Achieved Greatness
by Cathie Cush
Raintree Steck-Vaughn (1995)

Web Sites

Due to the changing nature of Internet links, PowerKids
Press has developed an online list of Web sites related
to the subject of this book. This site is updated regularly.
Please use this link to access the list:

http://www.powerkidslinks.com/wsh/kath/

Index

C
charities, 16
college, 6

J
journalism, 20

N
newsmagazine, 16

P
Personal History,
    18, 21
press, 20
Pulitzer Prize,
    18–19, 21

R
reporters, 12

S
stories, 4, 12, 14, 21

W
The Washington Post,
    6, 9–10, 16–17
Watergate Hotel,
    12–13
writer, 18

Word Count: 441

Note to Librarians, Teachers, and Parents

If reading is a challenge, Reading Power is a solution! Reading Power
is perfect for readers who want high-interest subject matter at an accessible reading
level. These fact-filled, photo-illustrated books are designed for readers who want
straightforward vocabulary, engaging topics, and a manageable reading experience.
With clear picture/text correspondence, leveled Reading Power books put the reader
in charge. Now readers have the power to get the information they want and the skills
they need in a user-friendly format.